Little Mitchie

LET'S LOOK INSIDE AN AIRPLANE

LET'S LOOK INSIDE: VEHICLES

PAUL ZACHARY

CREATING YOUNG NONFICTION READERS

Little Mitchie books spark curiosity and support early nonfiction reading for students in Grades 2-3. Designed to build vocabulary, support second language learners, and prepare readers for middle-grade content, each book includes helpful tips for parents and educators to build confidence and deepen understanding of the world.

TIPS FOR READING NONFICTION WITH BEGINNING READERS

Talk about Nonfiction

Begin by explaining that nonfiction books give us information that is true. The book will be organized around a specific topic or idea, and we may learn new facts through reading.

Look at the Parts

Most nonfiction books have helpful features. Our *Little Mitchie* titles include color photographs and graphic aids, a table of contents, a glossary, and an index. Share the purpose of these features with your reader.

Color Photos and Graphic Aids

A lot of information can be found by "reading" photos, charts, maps, and other graphic aids found within nonfiction texts. Help your reader learn more about the different ways information can be displayed.

Table of Contents

Located at the front of the book, this list shows the big ideas within the text and the page numbers where they can be found.

Glossary

Located at the back of the book, the glossary defines key words and phrases that are related to the topic. These words and phrases can be found in the text in colored type.

Index

Located at the back of the book, an index is an alphabetical list of topics and the page numbers where they can be found.

With a little help and guidance about reading nonfiction, you can feel good about introducing a young reader to the world of *Little Mitchie* nonfiction books.

Little Mitchie is an imprint of:

Mitchell Lane
PUBLISHERS

2001 SW 31st Avenue
Hallandale, FL 33009
mitchelllanepub.com

First Edition, 2027.

Author: Paul Zachary
Designer: Rhea Magaro
Editor: Tricia Hoffman

Library of Congress Cataloging-in-Publication Data
Title: Let's Look Inside an Airplane / by Paul Zachary.

Description: Hallandale, FL :
Mitchell Lane Publishers, [2027]

Identifiers:
ISBN 979-8-89260-883-1 (library bound)
ISBN 979-8-90145-052-9 (paperback)
ISBN 979-8-89260-986-9 (eBook)

Library of Congress Control Number: 2026930139

Photo credits: Shutterstock: Morozova Maria, 4; Rad K, 5; Kostiantyn Voitenko, 6; Morozova Maria, 7; Wasana Kunpol, 8; Kittyfly, 10; Chanawat Jaiya, 11; Morozova Maria, 12; APChanel, 13; Skycolors, 14; eric1207cvb, 17; Nafadh, 19; muratart, 21; narak0rn, 22

TABLE OF CONTENTS

Chapter One

LOOK UP!

Do you see that airplane flying high in the sky? Have you ever wondered what it's like inside? Let's take a trip and find out!

SKY-HIGH FACT
Airplanes fly so high that sometimes they are above the clouds.

Chapter Two

WHAT'S INSIDE?

The airplane door opens, and a smiling **flight attendant** says, "Welcome aboard!"

Inside the airplane are rows of seats and many small windows. Above our seats are overhead bins to store small bags. Suitcases are stored in a cargo area under the plane.

The seats are soft. There's a tray table that folds down so you can eat or color.

SKY-HIGH FACT

Before takeoff, flight attendants check the cabin to make sure everything is secured safely.

Above us are tiny lights, air vents, and buttons to call the flight attendant if we need help.

Our plane has small TVs on the backs of the seats in front of us! You can watch cartoons or play games.

Chapter Three

READY TO FLY

Once everyone is on board, the airplane begins to rumble. We sit tall and straight in our seats and make sure our seat belts are buckled.

The **jet engines** roar! The plane races down the **runway** before lifting into the sky. Up, up, up we go!

SKY-HIGH FACT
The wheels fold up inside the plane after it takes off.

SKY-HIGH FACT

Pilots use special radios to talk to air traffic controllers on the ground.

At the front of the plane is the **cockpit**. The cockpit is full of buttons, **levers**, and bright screens.

Two pilots sit in the cockpit and fly the plane. They wear uniforms and talk to the **control tower**.

In the back of the plane is the galley, where snacks and drinks are prepared. Flight attendants roll food and drink carts down the **aisle**. They pass out cookies, crackers, and other snacks to passengers who want them.

SKY-HIGH FACT

On longer flights, flight attendants heat meals in special ovens in the galley.

Need the bathroom? Don't worry! Airplanes have a tiny bathroom called a lavatory.

PUSH

Chapter Four

A SOFT LANDING

Soon the airplane begins to descend. The ground gets closer and closer as the plane flies lower.

When we land, the wheels bump the ground and the brakes slow us down. We roll to the gate. When the plane stops, the door opens once more. Time to grab our bags and explore this new city!

A LOOK INSIDE

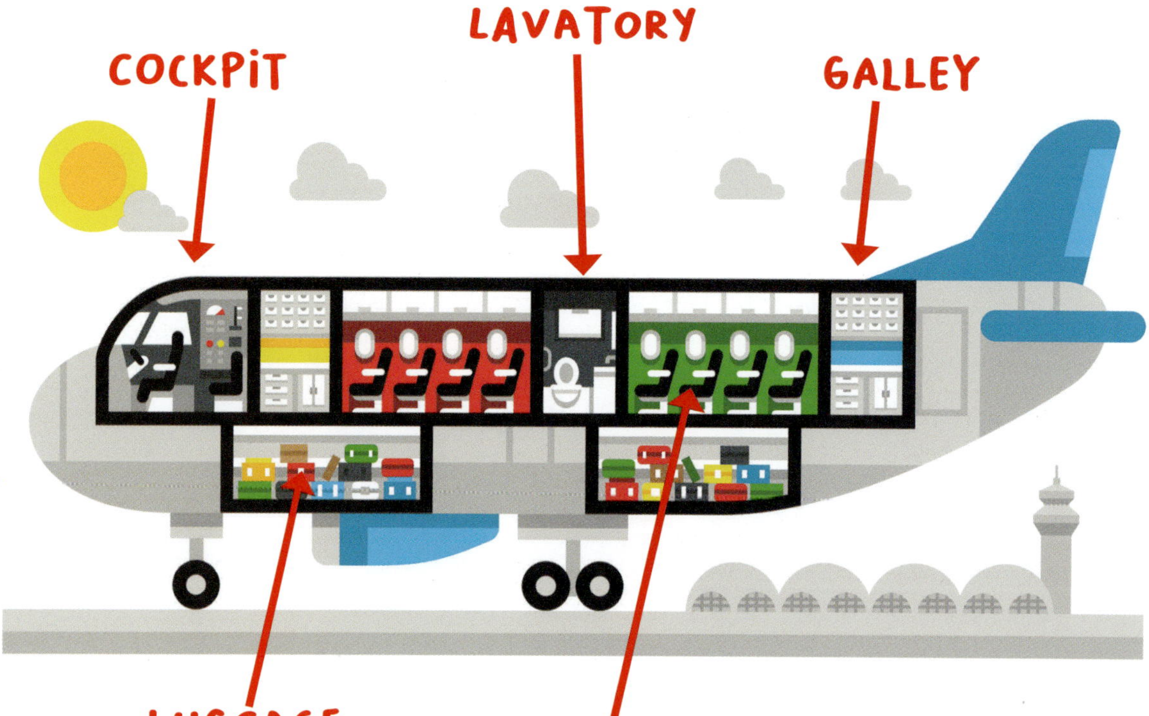

GLOSSARY

air traffic controller (air traf-ik kuhn-troh-lur) a person who helps guide airplanes safely in the sky and at airports

aisle (ile) the space between rows of seats where people walk

cockpit (kahk-pit) the control area in the front of a plane, where the pilot and sometimes the crew sit

control tower (kuhn-trohl tou-ur) a tall building at an airport where people guide airplanes during takeoff and landing

flight attendant (flite uh-ten-duhnt) a crew member who helps passengers and serves food and drinks on an airplane

jet engine (jet en-jin) a type of engine that pushes air backward to move the airplane forward

lever (lev-ur) a bar or handle that is pushed or pulled to make something move or work

runway (ruhn-way) a long strip of land where airplanes take off and land

FURTHER READING

Dittmer, Lori. *Airplanes.* The Creative Company, 2026.

Latham, Bethany. *Airplanes.* North Star Editions, 2026.

ON THE INTERNET

NASA Kids' Club
www.nasa.gov/learning-resources/nasa-kids-club/
Explore space, flight, and how aircraft travel through the air.

Smithsonian National Air and Space Museum
https://airandspace.si.edu/
See real airplanes and learn how flight works.

INDEX